Beer Making for the Total Novice

By Kyle Richards

Table of Contents

Introduction

Have you ever wondered how to brew beer at home? What kinds of ingredients are used? What type of equipment is needed? Is it expensive to get that equipment? Is it a difficult to do this, and how time consuming is it?

This book is for those the total novice to making beer. It answers these questions for you in clear, concise steps and walks you through how to make your own beer.

You will also learn interesting facts and history about beer to help equip you with even more knowledge of this new challenge.

Imagine serving your friends some amazing beer that you made yourself.

Enjoy the process, read on.

Some History of Beer

It was assumed, even by anthropologists, that when our fruit-gathering nomadic ancestors discovered the pleasure caused by drinking fermented fruit juices, they stopped moving around, planted crops, and drank beer. It is possible that this beverage was the reason why mankind formed communities and built civilizations.

The integration of beer and other fermented beverages into any civilization's culture is fascinating. What is more interesting is the fact that even in some of the oldest archaeological diggings ever found, evidence of beer jugs and even payment receipts were uncovered.

Social drinking is one of the oldest traditions still observed today. In fact, it can be argued that it is a foundation of many social activities and gatherings worldwide. From the celebration of a formal ceremony in a college kid's life to the success of a business enterprise, beer has been enjoyed.

Our literature is full of references to beer and other fermented drinks. It has been used as a basis for comparison, a metaphor or an analogy, or simply a statement of fact about humanity. Either in joy and sorrow, or in the stillness of a day, beer has lifted the hearts of men. In times of danger or great risk, it has helped stir courage and strengthen resolve. In times of war and in times of great peace, pubs and beer parlors have served as a secure place to wallow in one's feelings with a glass of beer.

Throughout the millennia embedded with the drink more than half the world enjoys, the commercialized, mass produced beer we drink today has gone through various evolutionary journeys. Perhaps we can tell the history of civilizations through the stages this beverage has been through. Perhaps we can account for all the tears shed, all the smiles that temporarily lit the world brighter, and all the sobs and laughter expressed in the presence of beer.

Around 9500 BC, also known as the early Neolithic period, ancient Iraq and ancient Egypt already had records indicating their attempts to have grains farmed. This makes it possible for beer historians to put the earliest date of beer production around that time. It was believed that the people of Sumer were fermenting a form of bread to make a fermented pulp that had a strong, intoxicating effect, called a "divine drink."

Ale, common in older times, is believed to have roots in the German, Finnish, Danish, and Norwegian tongues. The word "beer" is considered to have come from "bibere," a Latin word meaning "to drink." The word beer disappeared shortly during the Norman Conquest. It reappeared centuries later, pertaining to hopped malt beverages.

In Ebla, Syria, a discovery in 1974 showed that the city of Ebla produced a range of beers, including one that is named after the city. China was also a maker of fermented beverages based on the drink that was made of fermented fruit and wine, a discovery that was dated back to 7000 BC.

Germanic and Celtic tribes spread beer around 3000 BC, brewing it on a domestic scale. The Greeks learned the secret of brewing beer. The Greeks instructed the Romans how to brew beer. They called it "Cerevisia," a word deriving from the god of agriculture, Ceres, and "vis," the Latin word for strength. The Republican times displaced beer for wine as the alcoholic beverage. Beer was given to barbarians.

The addition on hops in the beer making process set a distinction in the 15th century, between beer and ale.

The term "lagers" surfaced accidentally in the 16th century when beers were kept in chilly caves for longer periods of time. Since then, ales were outpaced in terms of volume.

Before the Industrial Revolution, beer was produced on a domestic level until the 19th century, when brewing beer was set to industrial manufacturing.

Industrialization became a fact for making beer when the steam engine was invented in 1765. The hydrometer and thermometer in the 19th century allowed brew masters to further refine the brewing process.

Beer Facts And Myths

With thousands of years of history, it will not be surprising to find thousands of misconceptions about beer. It also does not mean that we know everything about it. Being familiar with something can cloud our judgment and at times makes us think that we do know everything there is to know about that topic. Take beer, for example.

Beer is one of the most widely consumed drinks and the third most popular drink in the world. It is produced in countless flavors and is produced in slightly different ways. Different factors make the beer unique, so every locality has the chance to stand out if research and experiments are done correctly.

Different civilizations have different perceptions about the value of beer. In Egyptian culture, beer is used for medical purposes and necessities in burials believed to sustain the departed in the journey from this life to the next. In courtship, when a man offers a woman a taste of his beer, it is already agreed that they are engaged.

In Rome, success in different missions meant a party and a toast together with their respected leaders, just like Caesar did when his troops crossed the Rubicon, which was the beginning of the Civil War of Rome.

Prior to the Middle Ages, beer brewing was left for the women to do as it was considered a household task.

Besides the fascinating facts about beer, the thousands of years of its history have generated some myths that are nothing but that – myths.

We commonly hear about people asking for sub-zero drinks, thinking that beer is at its best when it is very cold. In fact, warmth brings out the beer's flavor.

The color of the beer does not indicate anything about its alcohol content. It is commonly believed that dark beers have stronger alcohol content. All that needs to be done is to compare the labels of the bottle or can to see the actual alcohol content.

Beer making, also known as home brewing, is legal in the U.S. and many other places provided:

1. You annually produce only 100 gallons of beer (or less) by yourself; up to 200 gallons if you live in a household with another adult.

2. You do not sell your homemade beer.

3. You must be 21 or legal drinking age to make and drink your homebrew.

4. You may not distill hard alcohol.

5. You can taste and share homebrewed beer and wines.

Varieties of Beer

We can accept the fact that there are as many kinds of beer as there are brewers, and there are thousands of breweries today. One can't help but be surprised by the sheer number of beer choices in grocery stores. Every now and then, a new variety will appear on the shelves.

The level of temperature with which beer is produced determines which of the two major types of beer that particular beer falls under: ale or lager. Another factor is the yeast used in fermentation. Ale's yeast floats on top of the beer, while lager's yeast settles at the bottom.

Here is a list of the most common and widely produced beer:

Types of Ales - Ales are a type of beer that is tasty and sweet, coming in many different shades of color depending on the brewing procedure of the grains. They could be a deep, rich brown color ranging through to a light golden color.

Amber Ale – These taste a bit sweeter because of more malt and darker in color. They are considered Belgian Ale.

Pale Ale – This type is rich in hops and malt, and is lighter in color.

Bitter – Is a group that comes under the Pale Ales, containing hops for a very special scent.

Irish Ale – This type has a definite malt flavor and on the sweet side, and a deep reddish coloring.

Barley Wine – Contains a high alcohol content with a fruity flavor to it and is amber colored to nearly black.

Stouts – These beers are unique in that they are made with malt-free, dark roasted barley and limited hops. They come under the category of Dark Ales.

Porter – Brewed from a heavily roasted malt, these beers are very dark ales, having a crisp flavor and medium-bodied.

Wheat Beer – This type is very carbonated and light in color. Some names it is also known by is hfeweizen or weissbier.

Types of Lagers – These are made using a low temperature process during fermentation that gives a smooth, crisp taste.

Bock – This lager has a malt or hop flavor and is dark in color.

Dunkel – This German beer has a modest alcohol content, the color is dark.

Pale Lager – These beers are highly carbonated, light in color and possess a malt flavor.

Munich Dark Pale – This type has a blend of coffee and malt taste and is darker in color.

Dopple Bock – This type of beer is a malty and full bodied stronger version on Bock.

What Ingredients Do I Need?

1. Water

A great part of beer is made up of water. Although water is basically hydrogen and oxygen, water components in different regions play a role in the uniqueness of a beer.

2. Starch Source

This predicts the strength and flavor of the beer. The most commonly used starch in making beer is malted grain. Soaking the grain in water, which allows the beginning of germination, and then drying the grain in a kiln are done for the grain to be malted. Roasting time and temperature contribute to the colors of malt from the same grain.

3. Hops

Hop Bine's flower is utilized as both a preservative and a flavoring in most beer made now.

4. Yeast

Fermentation is caused by the yeast. It metabolizes sugar extracted from grains, producing alcohol and carbon dioxide. Yeast also contributes to character and flavor. A special type of yeast is used specifically for brewing beer, not the type used for baking bread.

An Overview of the Brewing Process

Brewing is the term for preparing (beer or ale) by steeping, boiling, and fermentation or by infusion and fermentation. Years ago, beer making was done at home and was a big part of domestic chores. Home brewing is the term used to describe beer production on a domestic scale, without regard to the location where it was made, although most home brewing is done at home.

Brewing converts the starch into a sweet liquid call wort. It then turns the wort into the alcoholic drink beer, by a process of fermentation by yeast.

A Basic Rundown

Mix the starch source with hot water. This is then mixed with malt in a mash tun. This stage can take up to two hours, in which starches are turned to sugars, and then drained from the grains. Sparging, sometimes known as lautering; allows the gathering of as much fermentable fluid from the grain as possible.

A kettle or large pot is where the wort is made and cooked. The water evaporates during the boiling, while the sugar and other components of wort remain. Hops are then added as a source of bitterness, flavor, and aroma.

After the boiling process, the wort must be quickly cooled. The yeast is then added to the mix. During fermentation, the wort turns into beer ranging in time from several days to several weeks. When the fermentation is done, yeast settles to the bottom of the fermenter vessel, creating a clarity in the beer.

Fermentation may be done in two stages known as primary and secondary. After the primary fermentation is done, the beer will be transferred to another container for the secondary fermentation. By using the secondary fermentation, it gives a greater clarity to the beer and is useful when the beer will be in storage for long periods. The beer is then bottled.

Terminologies To Know

The world of brewery is just like every other world, empire, or country. It has its own language. Jargons are necessary in different trades due to the fact that they make conversations quick-paced and understanding easier. Instead of taking the time to explain a long process, a word is enough to depict the whole idea.

Now, it will not hurt to know some of the widely used terminologies in the beer industry. Knowing them will make you appreciate the beloved drink, and also, it might be a good warm up conversation in beer pubs and other places.   It may also assist you if you start talking with others who make their own home brews.

Acrospire - When barley grain is germinated, acrospires are the shoots that grow.

Adjunct - This refers to any grain (usually corn or rice) or other ingredient that is fermentable in the process of brewing.

Amylase - Sometimes known as diastatic enzymes, this group is responsible for converting starches to sugars, largely in part comprising beta and alpha amylase.

Acrospire - When germinating barley, this is the tiny start of the plant shoot.

Aeration - In brewing, oxygen needs to be introduced to the wort during different stages to keep yeast healthy and for fermentation.

Aerobic - An oxygen using process.

Ale - A type of beer produced with a warm, short fermentation process usually from top fermenting yeast.

Alcohol by Volume (ABV)

The alcohol content measurement. To do this:

Subtract the final gravity from the original gravity and divide by 0.0075. For example: $1.050 - 1.012 = 0.038/0.0075 = 5\%$ ABV.

Alcohol by Weight (ABW)

A measurement of the alcohol content of a solution in terms of the percentage weight of alcohol per volume of beer. This measurement is always lower than the alcohol by volume. To calculate the approximate alcohol content by weight, subtract the final gravity from the original gravity and divide by 0.0095. For example: $1.050 - 1.012 = 0.038/0.0095 = 4\%$ ABW.

Alpha Acid Units (AAU) - A specific measure of hops, multiplied by a certain percentage of alpha acids.

Aldehyde - A precursor chemically to alcohol and at times produces flavors that are off.

Alkalinity - A PH measurement of a substance ranging between 7 and 14. A main cause of this in brewing water is from bicarbonate ion.

Aleurone Layer - In barley corn, this is the living covering of the endosperm that contains enzymes.

Amino Acids - Made up of organic acid in the amine group, amino acids are building blocks of protein.

Amylopectin - In barley, it's found in the endosperm and is a starch chain, made of amylose.

Amylose - This is also found in the endosperm of barley and is a straight chain molecule.

Anaerobic - A method that uses no oxygen or even may be dependent of the total absence of it.

Autolysis - When yeast cells die, the insides release into the beer creating an unpleasant taste.

Attenuation - The amount of conversion of sugar to carbon dioxide and alcohol.

Beerstone - A tough metallic, scaly, deposit that forms on fermentation equipment that is mostly calcium oxalate.

Biotin - Found in yeast, liver and egg yolks, biotin is a crystalline of vitamin B complex.

Blow-off - An airlock type system that allows carbon dioxide to be released as well as extra fermentation matter.

Buffer - A chemical type, that helps to stabilize the pH of a liquid. Salt is a good example.

Cellulose - Close to a starch, except made in an opposite direction, it can't be degraded by starch enzymes, or the other way around.

Cold Break - Thickening proteins drop out of the liquid when wort is quickly cooled before pitching the yeast.

Conditioning - This process is done during the secondary fermentation and continues when after bottled as well. It is when the yeast further refines the taste of the near-completed beer.

Decoction - This is a process of mashing to create rests in temperature by boiling some of the boil, then adding that back to the rest of the mash trub.

Dextrin - After a diastatic enzyme action on a starch, dextrin is a complex sugar molecule that is left.

Dextrose - Similar to glucose yet it's molecular structure is the mirror opposite of glucose.

Diastatic Power - In malt, this would be degree of diastatic enzyme potential that is present.

Dimethyl Sulfide (DMS) - This is a flavor desired in small amounts in lagers.

Enzymes - Enzymes are protein catalysts that have biochemical activity.

Endosperm - The nutrition portion of a seed containing lipids, proteins and carbohydrates.

Esters - Fragrant substances made from alcohols due to yeast action.

Ethanol - This is the kind of alcohol found in beer that is made from malt sugars by the yeast.

Fermentation - The complete transformation of malt sugars into beer.

Finings - Substances that help the yeast clump together and settle out of completed beer. These might be Irish moss, isinglass or bentonite as examples.

Flocculation - A term for yeast grouping together and settling out of the finished beer.

Fructose - Sometimes known as fruit sugar. It is different from glucose in that has a ketone group instead of an aldehydic carbonyl component.

Fusel Alcohol - This type carry a strong, almost chemical taste and believed to be somewhat responsible for causing hangovers. It is an alcohol that posses higher weight molecules that esterify in typical conditions.

Gelatinization - A method that makes starches soluble with water by either enzyme action, heat or both.

Germination - During the malting process, this is when the acrospire begins to grow and emerges from the hull.

Glucose - A single, most basic sugar molecule.

Glucanase - This is an enzyme found in the endosperm of oatmeal, wheat and unmalted barley.

Gravity - Refers to the degree of malt sugar in the wort.

Grist - Crushed malt before the mashing process.

Hardness - Water hardness equals the density or magnesium ions and dissolved calcium, and usually written as ppm.

Hydrolysis - The method of decomposition of some type of chemical in water, by either biochemical or chemical action.

Hops - A plant vine used to make beer. The cone shaped flowers are used and may be whole, in plugs or pellets.

Hopback - A container that functions as a filter to remove break material from the completed wort, and is filled with hops.

Hot Break - Refers to proteins that gel and drop from solutions during the boiling process of the wort.

Hot Water Extract - An international unit representing the total soluble extra of a malt.

Infusion - A type of mashing method where heating is done through the additions of more boiling water.

International Bittering Units (IBU) - A unit for measuring hops that is precise.

Invert Sugar - A combination of fructose and dextrose in fruits, or created artificially.

Isinglass - A protein collagen that absorbs yeast through electrostatic binding.

Irish Moss - Serves as an emulsifying substance that helps break material formation while boiling and cooling.

Krausen

A German term that refers to the foam that develops on a beer when it undergoes its most aggressive period of fermentation, krausen is another word you will never miss in beer talks.

Lactose - A milk sugar that is non-fermentable, and sometimes added to a stout beer.

Lager - This type of beer is made from bottom fermenting yeast with a long cooling process.

Lag Phase - This is the time of rapid yeast growth upon pitching to the wort, usually two to twelve hours in duration.

Lautering

The method of extracting wort from the whole grain after mashing is called lautering.

Lipid - Is a structural component of a live cell, and are soluble in organic liquids. These might be waxes, phosphatides, fats and other related substances.

Liquor

This is not about any beverage with alcohol content. This is not gallons of whiskey or a bottle of bourbon. In the world of beer brewers, water is referred to as liquor. When heated, it is then referred to as 'hot liquor.'

Lupulin Glands - On the base of hop petals, there are tiny yellow nodes that contain the resins used in brewing beer.

Maillard Reaction - This is a reaction from heat when an amino acid and a sugar form a complex that causes browning.

Maltose - A popular food for brewing yeast.

Mash - This is the hot water method that helps with the breakdown of grist to fermentable, soluble sugars.

pH - A scale that reveals alkalinity or acidity of a substance. 7 is neutral, 14 most alkaline, and 1 is most acidic.

PPM - Stands for parts per million, equaling milligrams per liter.

Peptidase - An enzyme that creates amino acids by breaking up proteins in the endosperm.

Pitching - The process of adding yeast to the fermenter.

Protease - An enzyme that breaks larger proteins in the endosperm that is responsible for causing haze in a beer.

Phenol, Polyphenol - This hydrocarbon can result in medicinal tastes in beer and a stale flavor.

Primary Fermentation - This is the first fermentation cycle, much of the total attenuation happens at this point.

Priming - Right before bottling, priming is adding a small quantity of fermentable sugar to the beer, to give carbonation.

Racking - Is siphoning beer away from the trub as gently as possible.

Secondary Fermentation - This is the phase after the primary fermentation is completed, yet before the bottling process. It is a time when the beer is conditioning and settling.

Sparging

Once the sweet wort is drained from the grain after mashing, sparging occurs. It is a small part of a much bigger process called lautering. When there is still a huge amount of good fermentable sugars sitting on the grain, the brewer sprays water over the grain bed to rinse some of it off. That process is called sparging.

Sterols - These are solid steroid alcohols found in animal or plant lipids.

Sucrose - A molecule consisting of a fructose and glucose joined together.

Tannins - Compounds found in hop cones and grain husks.

Trub (or troob) - This is the sediment found at the bottom of a fermenter.

Wort

You can't miss this word in every brewer's work. Simply put, wort is the term used for the beer before the fermentation process. Wort is to beer what a cocoon is to a butterfly. All the hard work remains as plain wort until the yeast does its job.

What Kind of Equipment Do I Need?

Besides the common terms that a want-to-be brewer should know, it is imperative that a beginner be at ease with the list of the most common equipment used in the brewing process. Fortunately most of the equipment is not very expensive. Some folks opt to purchase a beer making kit, while others choose to buy the components individually. Below is a list of the various equipment parts you will need.

Airlock

These small device allows fermentation gas to escape while keeping oxygen out.

Boiling Pot

Any large pot capable of holding at least 3 gallons of liquid, it might be aluminum, ceramic coated steel or stainless steel. You can also go a route of buying a pot with a built in thermometer, specifically made for brewing beer.

Bottles

For a typical 5 gallon batch, at least 48 12 oz bottles that are re-cappable, or you can use larger bottles if you want.

Bottle Caps

Standard or oxygen absorbing caps are available in most homebrewing stores, if you do not use bottles that are re-cappable.

Bottle Capper

These are a small hand tool to secure the bottle caps on bottles.

Bottle Brush

A long handled brush is needed to cleaning the beer bottles.

Bottle Filler

A tube made of metal or rigid plastic, many a spring loaded valve is at the top to help fill the beer bottles.

Fermenter

A food-grade 6 gallon plastic bucket is perfect to use for this purpose.

Glass Jar

At least capable of holding 12 ounces of liquid.

Pyrex Measuring Cup

Pyrex measuring cups are great for handling boiling water and other ingredients. You can use whatever suits you, but make sure it can handle boiling water.

Racking Cane

Is a plastic tube system that helps to keep the bottom sediment behind when siphoning beer into bottles.

Sanitizer

This is so important to successful brewing, there will be a whole chapter dedicated to this topic.

Siphon

Another very inexpensive tool, used to transfer your beer during various stages of brewing.

Stirring Paddle

This is a paddle used to stir the wort during the boiling process. Must be food-grade plastic or wood materials.

Tablespoon

You'll need a metal tablespoon for measuring.

Thermometer

You will need a thermometer that has a range of minimally 40 degrees - 180 degrees F. Ideally a floating type or one that can be immersed is best.

Optional but Highly Recommended

Bottling Bucket

This would be a food-grade 6 gallon plastic bucket with a spigot. By siphoning finished beer into this bucket before bottling, allows you to bottle with the spigot instead of a bottle filler. It may help produce beer with less sediment in the finished bottles.

Hydrometer

This is an instrument used to gauge the process of fermentation when beer is made from scratch. It's usually not necessary however for first-time brewers, who usually are using a standard recipe.

Turkey Baster

These are used to draw small samples from the wort without contaminating the whole batch.

What About Sanitization?

Sanitization is critically important in beer brewing, it is a very attractive environment for bacteria, molds and wild yeast to grow. If these get into your beer at any point, the beer will be ruined. This is probably THE most important aspect to successful beer brewing there is. If you are going to go through the process to make beer, you want to ensure that you do it correctly, and this is the correct foundation; properly sanitized conditions.

While there are many methods and options available to clean and sanitize equipment, I'm going to keep it simple and use my favorite methods, but will offer several options.

Cleaning and sanitization are not the same thing. You are looking at a two step process. Cleaning is the removal of dirt, grime and residue that is usually visible to the eye and needs to be removed before sanitizing. It is the first step in the process.

Sanitizing is the process of treating your equipment chemically, that not only eradicates but helps prevent the growth of wild yeasts, bacteria and molds.

At every point in your beer making endeavor, be sure to wash and scrub your hands thoroughly with hot water and soap. Before starting you beer making, you need to clean and sanitize every part of every single item that will come into contact with your beer process, including turkey baster, airlocks, auto-siphons, jars, tubes, stirrers, plastic buckets, thermometers, bottles and caps, everything that has to do with the process in any way. A good wipe down of the surface areas you will be working on is also important.

For the first cleaning step, I like to use a chemical cleaner with a soak, then gently scrub the parts I can. The reason I prefer this is some parts in an airlock or other pieces can be difficult to reach for a good scrub, and yet this gets them clean.

Both products recommended are called percarbonates, which are a blend of hydrogen peroxide and sodium carbonate and other ingredients. They work with a mild alkali and active oxygen to lift dirt and grime. They are also easy on the septic system and environmentally friendly. P.B.W. use 2 oz. in 5 gallons of warm water, soak your equipment for 30 minutes, then rinse. Straight A cleanser use at 1 Tablespoon per gallon of water, soak for 30 minutes, then rinse. This is also good for removing labels off glass.

Next you will need to sanitize all your equipment. This can be done immediately after cleaning if desired. Although chlorine may be used, very thorough rinsing is critical and if it's not properly rinsed everywhere, it could ruin your beer. The sanitizers listed below are all very reasonably priced and worth not having to be so critical on rinsing.

Campden tablets are potassium metabisulfite and is an excellent sanitizer of your beer equipment, again this means all items. If you buy the tablet form, simple crush with a mortar & pestle into a fine powder, or you can purchase the powdered form. Mix 8 teaspoons per 1 gallon a water, allow your equipment to soak for 5 minutes, then allow to drip dry. No rinsing needed.

A second method for sanitizing is with an iodine product called Iodophor. Its used in both the medical industry and food service to sanitize equipment. Make a solution of 1 Tablespoon per gallons of water, then soak all equipment for 10 minutes, then drip dry. No rinsing necessary. This will stain fabric however, so you will need to be careful about that.

Another popular option is a product called Star-San, this foams readily getting into cracks and crevices, odorless, flavorless and biodegradable. Will not affect your beer negatively in any way.

Mix 1 ounce per 5 gallons of water, soak your equipment for 1 minutes, then drip dry. No rinsing needed.

Now that all your equipment is gathered, cleaned and sanitized, you are ready to begin. You will want to ensure that you have all your food ingredients on hand as well, coming up next.

How to Brew Your Own Beer

Beer brewing does not begin and end with a brewing kit. Neither does reading how it is done accomplish anything – besides acquiring knowledge, that is. In order for a person to brew beer, he or she actually needs to get started.

The following chapter will help you get over that overwhelming feeling and get started with your dream of brewing your own beer. The whole process can be divided into three main events or steps: brewing, fermentation, and bottling. It is recommended to read this section over prior to brewing your beer, as there will be more explanations in this section than a typical recipe contains.

Once you have everything sanitized, have thoroughly washed your hands, and have all your materials gathered, you are ready to begin!

Brewing Your First Batch

Recipe for a Pale Beer:

Ingredients for a 5 gallon batch:

- 5 gallons of bottled drinking water (not distilled)

- 5-7 pounds of Pale Malt Extract syrup, hopped

- 1-2 ounces of Hops (optional for more hop flavor)

- 1 packet of dry Ale yeast

- 3/4 cup honey or corn sugar

- Spray bottle filled with bottled drinking water

Gather the ingredients

Check whether you have everything you need. If you bought a kit, you still need to check whether the extract is hopped or if it is there at all.

In the absence of a kit, visit the nearest homebrew store and look for the things outlined in the recipe provided, or order online.

Boil water

A gallon of sterile water is needed for a variety of small tasks. Begin by boiling about a gallon of water for 10 minutes and letting it cool to room temperature. Keep it covered.

Prepare the Wort

In your large pot bring 2 1/2 gallons of bottled drinking water to boil. While waiting for this to happen, re-hydrate your dry yeast (see section below this).

After the water has boiled, remove from heat then add all the malt syrup and stir until completely dissolved, being mindful to include the syrup that would want to stick to the bottom of the pot. You don't want this to burn as it would give a burnt sugar 'off' taste to your beer.

This next phase is vital! Put the pot back onto the stove and bring to a rolling boil. Stir frequently, and start your timer for 1 hour. If you are adding hops (bittering type), add them now.

You might begin to see a foam form with a smooth surface, which is a good sign. If it quickly rises up and boils over the pot, not a good thing. Adding the hops may trigger this boil over, so you need to watch it carefully. The wort is very unstable now and will be for up to 20 minutes, when the wort stops foaming (sometimes called Hot

Break). A couple things you can do to avoid the boil over is reduce the heat somewhat, but you still need to keep the rolling boil going. Another tactic to try is to gentle spray the foam with the water from a spray bottle.

Stir occasionally during this 1 hour rolling boil. It may change in both smell and color, that is normal. If you plan to add finishing hops (optional), add it in the last 15 minutes of this hour rolling boil.

Re-hydrate Dried Yeast

Rehydration of yeast guarantees the best results. Put a cup of warm (95-105°F, 35-40°C), pre-boiled water into your sanitized jar and stir in the yeast. Cover with plastic wrap and wait 15 minutes.   Add 1 teaspoon or honey, malt extract or sugar then gently stir. Keep it out of direct sunlight. There should be signs of foaming or churning.

Cooling the Wort

It is critical to get the wort cooled quickly to below 80 degrees F. By doing so, it helps prevent contamination or oxidation, both of which can ruin your beer. It also will prevent your beer from getting an odd vegetable type taste.

Take your hot wort (carefully), off the stove and put in a sink or bathtub filled with ice water, being careful not to let the water fall into the pot. Swirl the cold water gently around the pot to help cool it rapidly.   If the water gets warm, drain some and add more ice. You can the wort to hit 80 degrees in 20 minutes.

Starting the Fermentation Process

Put the other 2 1/2 gallons of bottled drinking water into your bucket fermenter. Now pour the cooled wort into the fermenter, allowing splashing and churning, that will help to provide oxygen the yeast will need now to reproduce. Check the temperature now, you want it to be between 65 - 75 degrees F.

Pitching the Yeast

Add all of your jar of re-hydrated yeast into the wort now. Stir thoroughly with your stir paddle. Put the lid on the bucket and seal it. Fill your airlock to the line with sterile water (you boiled at first) and insert into the hole of the fermenting bucket.

Primary Fermentation Process

This primary fermentation process will begin within twelve hours and you'll see and hear the airlock bubbling. If using liquid yeast, it could be up to 24 hours.

Place the fermenting bucket in a safe, stable place away from children and pets. A bathtub or shower is a good place because if foam runs out, it's easy to clean up. Keep it at a constant temperature preferably between 65 - 75 degrees, try not to allow it to get above 80 degrees.

It may ferment slowly or quickly; but whichever rate is fine. The trick is giving enough active yeast. Some very active ferments may be done as soon as 3 days (sometimes it stops, then re-starts again), a slower one may take up to a couple of weeks. If the foam pops the airlock out of place, rinse the airlock with bleach water, wipe off the lid and return the airlock to the lid. When bubbling has slowed, do not lift the lid to peak, as the beer is still vulnerable to infections that could ruin it. It's totally acceptable to leave it alone for 2 - 3 weeks. Allowing more time before bottling allows more time for sediment to settle resulting in a clearer beer. It also give more 'finishing' time yielding a better beer.

Some folks opt for a secondary fermentation process, basically siphoning the beer out of the primary fermenting bucket into a sanitized new one, attaching a new airlock and allowing to further 'condition' up to 2 more weeks. This however is optional, and may be something you may want to try after you've got one or two batches successfully made.

Priming and Bottling Your Brew

When the primary fermentation has stopped (2 - 3 weeks), it is ready to bottle. There shouldn't be bubbles in the airlock, or very few. If beer is bottled too soon, it can become over-carbonated and at times even cause a bottle to explode. Not fun.

Have your bottles, caps and all equipment washed and sanitized. Do not heat bottle caps.

Boil 3/4 cup of either corn sugar or 1 1/4 dry malt extract in 1/2 cup water, then allow it to cool. Open the lid to the fermenter and carefully pour this priming mixture into the beer. Stir gently with the paddle, trying not to stir up the sediment on the bottom. Wait half an hour for the sediment to settle and the priming solution to work.

You will now begin to siphon your beer into the bottles. Be careful not to have the end of the siphon touch the bottom of the bucket, as you don't want to siphon that bottom sediment into your beer bottles. Do not suck on the hose to start the siphon, it will contaminate your beer. Put the other end of the siphon hose to the bottom of the beer bottle and slowly fill to 3/4 of the bottle. Pinch the flow, then keep filling the remaining bottles. Cap the bottles and inspect to make sure they are properly sealed.

Store your capped, finished beer at room temperature for two weeks before serving. If you chill the beer before serving, some batches may have a 'chill haze' and is nothing to worry about. Congratulations!

Record Keeping

Observation is the key to perfection. The best products we enjoy today started as experiments that were done over and over again, making the necessary adjustments to come up with the right ratio and methods that will produce the best results. All of these are impossible to accomplish without keen observation and good record keeping.

The test of a skilled brewer is to repeat the good batches that were produced and learn from the failed batches. An organized recipe will help determine the factors that contribute to the outcome of the batch. It will also serve as a point of reference in everything that will be needed in gathering the conditions produce a certain effect.

Good record keeping keeps you upbeat and productive. It makes you grow and opens unlimited possibilities for the batches you will produce in the future.

The process of home brewing beer can be quite complex, especially as you begin to add in more ingredients or steps to your process. Many folks begin with a simple process like we've outlined here, and then begin to move up to make other types of beer and master new skill levels. Literally the options are limitless in what can be created.

Be sure to record all failures too, because those will help you to avoid the same mistakes in future batches.

For many folks, this first batch of beer is the beginning of a life-long hobby.

What Is Malt?

Malted barley is the key to producing beer. The sugar fermented from malted barley is what the beer is made from. Malt is an abbreviation for maltose.

When barley is soaked and drained to initiate the germination of the plant from the seed, the malting process begins. Once the seed germinates, enzymes are activated that convert its starch into sugars and amino acids. These enzymes are then used by the brewer.

To accelerate enzyme activity, the malted barley is crushed and soaked in hot water, thus converting the barley's reserve starch into sugars in a very short amount of time. This sugar is boiled with hops and then fermented with yeast to produce beer.

In general, for every gallon of water used to make a light bodied beer, you'll need 1 pound of malt extract syrup. For a richer-bodied beer, use 1 1/2 pounds per gallon of water.

By using a ready-made malt extract, it makes the process of beer brewing much simpler for the beginner. It can be purchased in either a powdered form or a syrup. It is also sold as either hopped or un-hopped.

If using a hopped variety of malt extra, a person doesn't have to add any more hops to the beer, but may want to anyway for a more pronounced hop flavor. If using an un-hopped malt extract, then 1 - 2 ounces of hops will need to be added to the wort.

In an extremely over-simplified note about hops, there are two major categories. Aroma and Bittering hops. The bittering hops are used at the beginning of the wort boiling process, while aroma hops are considered a finishing hop and added to the boiling wort solution anywhere from the last 5 to 15 minutes of the boil. This is a subject that whole books can be written on, and can get complex quickly.

Some home brewers decide to develop their skill of mashing. That is extracting their own malt sugars from the whole grain. This opens up a whole new realm of brewing.

Common Mistakes Beginners Make

Brewing can be a very exciting activity in your life. Besides the fact that you will get to enjoy your end product, you have a craft you can be proud of. However, many enthusiasts are overcome by the failures of the first batch they brew.

The following are some of the common mistakes that can happen.

Inadequate Sanitation

Cleanliness is the correct foundation of successful brewing. The fastest way to a spoiled batch is to not follow this rule. The word rule was used, not advice. It is a must-do, not an option.

Failure to Follow the Recipe

The whole process of brewing is quick-paced. Unfamiliarity with the instructions will definitely lead to confusion and the possibility of skipping what seems an irrelevant step, like double-checking whether the stirrer is sanitized. Make sure that the steps are followed in order and that measures of the substances needed are accurate.

Skip Kindergarten

You can't expect a first grader to compute complicated algebraic equations and get them right. Beer brewing goes thousands of years back. There are basic steps you need to know well before you can pursue the more complicated brews. Begin with easy brews. Get to know the process by heart. Only when you have enjoyed and mastered the basic brews should you move on to try brewing other beers.

Impatience

Nobody likes to wait for their beer, especially on a bad day. Your beer will need at least 1-2 weeks in the primary and 1 week or longer in the secondary if you're using one. It's tough to be patient, but the results will be better. Also, it can take 1-2 weeks or longer for your beer to carbonate in the bottle.

Being a Cheapskate

You will never save money on stale ingredients unless you are in for a stale finished result. Get to know your homebrew stores and read labels.

Keeping the Pot on the Hot Stove

This applies when you are adding the malt extract. Stir the malt extract evenly. Removing the brew pot from the heat prevents the malt extract from getting stuck on the bottom of the pot, getting burned, and adding bad burnt flavors to your brew.

Leaving the Wort Unattended

The wort knows when you're not around. Kind of. If you don't want the wort boiling over and creating a mess all over the stove, you'd better keep an eye on this treacherous substance.

Keeping the Brew Pot Lid On

Besides the fact that it speeds up the increase in the wort's temperature, keeping the lid on deters chemicals that are determined enough to give your beer off-tasting flavors and aromas. So, keep it uncovered while cooking.

Oxidizing Your Brew

In yeast preparation, you have to make it a point that the wort has as much oxygen as it needs. However, after that point, you have to be careful not to expose it to oxygen any longer.

Not Keeping Records

Unless you are certain that you are capable of remembering the small details that affect your production, taking notes will be needed. The beer we enjoy today have gone through various stages before they reached mass production. The slight change in temperature, the variety of yeast, and other factors were observed keenly.

Most importantly, keeping records is the easiest way for a brewer to track down his or her growth. You are closer to the brew you have in mind when things are done with order and organization.

Here are a few problems you should watch out for in your beer. Contamination can happen at any point of the process and isn't always easy to detect.   In general, if the beer can be consumed easily it won't cause physical problems.   If your brew has any of the following signs however, toss it out.

1. 1. If the bottled beer possesses a milky appearance at the top and/or residue clumps sticking on the sides of the bottle neck in the air space   area.   The beer will smell rotten and taste terrible. Don't confuse it   however is a dew that forms near the bottle cap, this is normal.

2. 2.   If there is mold on top of the beer, or slimy strands in the beer,   toss it out.

3. If it has an animal - musk type scent, toss it. This is due to light damaging the beer. It needs to be stored in dark areas.

4. If the bottled beer's quality is getting worse with age. If it seems stale, or has a sherry type flavor, oxidation has happened. Next time consume it sooner.

5. If the bottled beer starts to smell really sweet, similar to molasses. This is an indication that it is beginning to turn into a malt vinegar.

Conclusion

Learning a craft can both be fulfilling and frustrating. In fact, it is this part that determines a casual new-thing-seeker from a real, authentic enthusiast. When you go beyond the frustrations, you will discover a new world. You'll see a drawback as an opportunity and spoiled batches as a forward step to growth and success in the future.

Brewing your own beer can begin as a hobby done in the course of the free hours you have. However, it will not hurt to work, take the process to heart, and spend your time in this pursuit.

The world of brewing is like discovering new places in the city where you grew up. It is the unraveling of the new things from what we have already seen and done.

With brewing your own beer, you will not only appreciate the beverage more, but also the method it took to make it.

Most importantly, never neglect that it is fascinating and fun to finally customize your beer. With a few tweaks and practice, you will get hooked on this craft, and sooner or later, find yourself up for the challenge, ready for the pursuit of a better brew. There are literally hundreds of recipes that can be tried.

If you enjoyed this book or received value from it in any way, would you be kind enough to leave a review for this book on Amazon? I would be so grateful. Thank you!